Mandalas Created for the World and Humanity

Gail Alexander

IbbiLane Press

Copyright © 2016

All rights reserved. No part of this book may be reproduced or utilized in any form or by any means, electronic or mechanical, including photocopying, recording, or by any information storage and retrieval systems without the permission in writing from the publisher.

Cover design by the author.

ISBN-13: **978-0692762493 (IbbiLane Press)**

ISBN-10: 0692762493

Dedication:

To my fellow human beings, we are all in this together. No one gets out alive. Let's create a reality of peace on earth.

Acknowledgements

Thank you to my family and friends. A special thank you to my uncle Michael.

Thank you to my publisher Kellie for trusting my vision and guidance.

Lastly and certainly not least thank you to my Guides, Angels, Arch Angels, Ascended Masters and Multi-Dimensional Beings for the gift of the Mandalas. I am grateful and appreciative.

Table of Contents

Introduction	9
Golden Pink Light Meditation	11
Mandalas Created for the World	13
Angel Mandalas for Humanity and the World	29
Mandalas of Peace and Love	45
Mandalas for Humanity	63
Mandala Codes for the World and Humanity	79
Epilogue	95

Introduction:

I felt compelled to create this book of Mandalas to send energy to the world and humanity during these difficult times. There has been so much death, violence and unease. We are at a precipice right now and humanity needs to make some decisions as to which way we wish to go. We are all being called upon to work through old and new issues so we can fully be here now to take our place and help with the shift that is happening.

I have drawn and created all the mandalas in this book by hand; they are not computer generated. I have left the imperfections in, as that is how the originals look. I did enhance them by putting a glow of silver or gold around the image to help the image stand out a little. I have removed the names of the mandalas, as I would like the images to be used intuitively and instinctively. Everyone who looks at them will get, see or feel something different, as we all have different frequencies, vibrations, and our own unique point of view. The mandalas can be used as transmitters or receivers, whichever you need at the time.

I have broken the book down into five sections. The first section is about sending energy out to the world whenever anything happens. There is so much going on in the world right now. These mandalas can be used for any event that happens. The second section is about receiving help from the other side and then sending that energy back out into the world and to humanity. The third section is all about peace and love. We all need to be able to give as well as receive. The fourth section is about humanity and all of us coming together to bring about the changes we wish to see in the world and helping to create a new reality for all. The fifth and last section are codes for the world. These mandalas will help with accessing ancient and future knowledge, the power of the sun, water, DNA and the cosmos.

The book can be used sequentially where you start in the beginning and look through all the images in order. Or you can just let the book fall open and work with that mandala. Again the only thing that will appear is the names of the sections the rest is open to your own interpretation and guidance.

I have written a meditation to use if so guided to help bring in love and knowledge.

The Golden Pink Light Meditation

Sit quietly for a few minutes and focus on breathing in and out. Just be present and have an awareness of your breath going in and out.

Now imagine that a golden pink light is above your head and slowly filling your crown chakra with this amazing, vibrant light. Let the top of your head be filled with the light and see it glowing a golden pink color.

As you continue to be aware of your breath the golden pink light now moves down to your third eye chakra in the middle of your forehead. The whole top of your head is now glowing with golden pink light. Filling and illuminating your third eye with golden pink light.

As you continue to be aware of your breath the golden pink light travels down to your throat chakra and your whole head, throat and neck are glowing with golden pink light. You start to feel your thoughts disappear as you embrace the golden pink light. You feel yourself more present in the moment.

Again as you become aware and focused on your breath the golden pink light moves down to your heart chakra in the middle of your chest and goes down your arms all the way to your finger tips. The whole top third of your body is glowing with the golden pink light filling you with love and knowledge and wisdom. You feel peaceful and serene as the golden pink light fills you up.

As you breathe the golden pink light travels down to your solar plexus chakra or stomach area filling all cells, organs, structures, and blood in your body with the golden pink light. You feel peaceful and centered as every part of your body starts to light up with the golden pink light.

As you continue to breathe the golden pink light travels down to your sacral chakra halfway between your belly button and the base of your spine.   Again filling every nook and cranny.

Again your breath moves the golden pink light down to your root chakra at the base of your spine. The golden pink light travels down your legs out the bottom of your feet and goes all the way down to the center of the earth to the Earth Mother who is waiting to receive this gift of golden pink light from above. In return the Earth mother sends up earth energy for you and the universe and it travels all the way through the earth through the bottom of your feet, up your legs, up your legs, your body and spinal column and shoots up through your crown chakra to the universe.

You are now connected above and below and are a vessel of divine love and wisdom. Now look through the mandalas and work with them from this space.

Mandalas Created for the World

Angel Mandalas for Humanity and the World

40

Mandalas of Peace and Love

Mandalas for Humanity

Mandala Codes for the World and Humanity

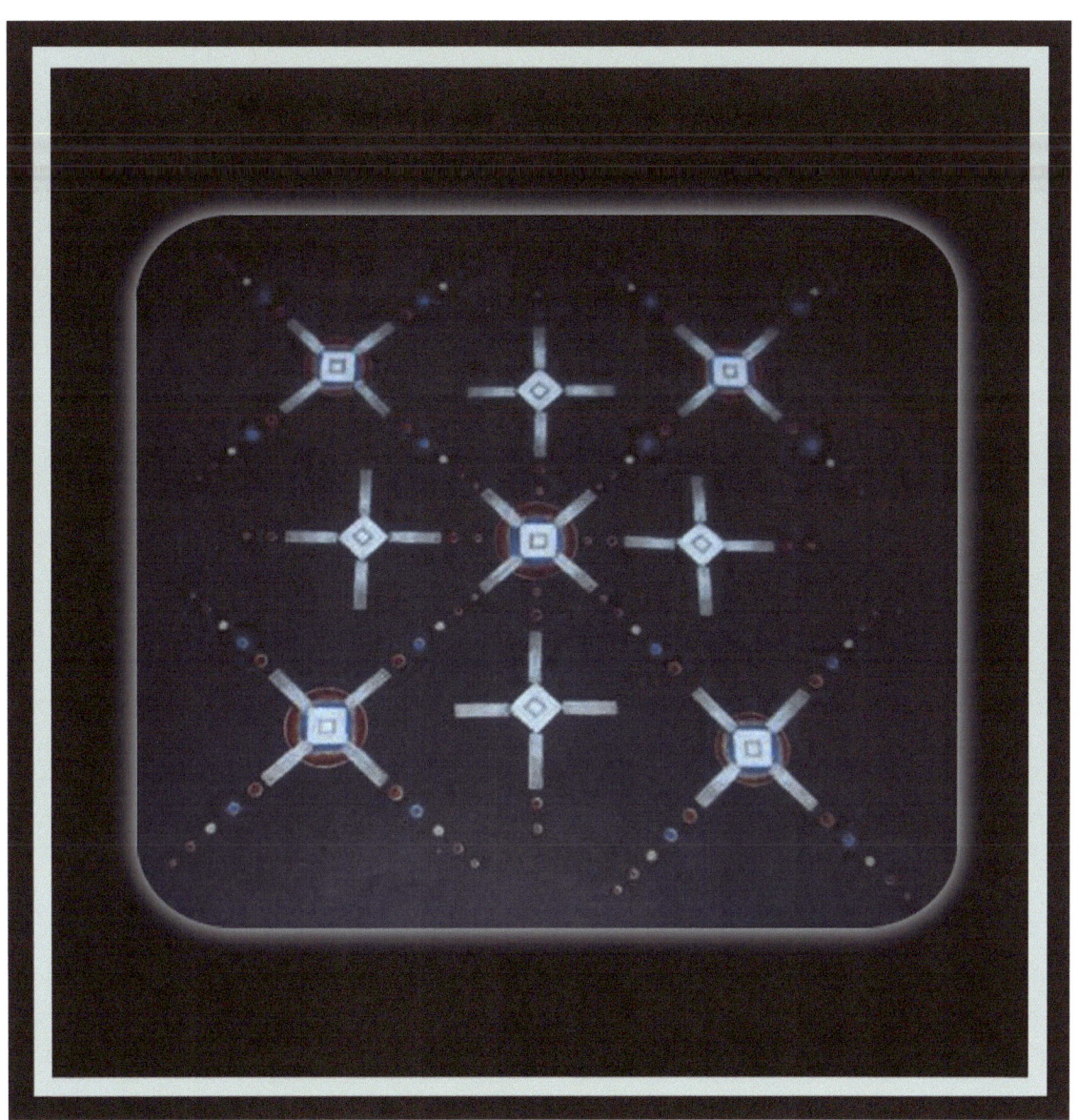

Epilogue

Thank you for picking up this book and for sending and receiving energy working with the mandalas. We are all one. Don't underestimate what you can do to help. It takes all of us playing our parts to make change. It is time that we all start to remember this. There is no separation.

Namaste!

www.ingramcontent.com/pod-product-compliance
Lightning Source LLC
Chambersburg PA
CBHW042139290426
44110CB00002B/57